GOING FOR GOLD

At the ancient Olympic Games, the winning competitors were awarded a simple crown made of olive branches. At the modern Olympics, the winners are rewarded with medals made of solid gold.

Olympic commemorative medal, 1896

EXCELLENCE IN ACTION

Competitors with disabilities have excelled at power and precision events such as archery, shooting, and horse riding. In 1952, Lis Hartel (DEN) became the first woman to win a medal in the dressage event, even though she was partially paralyzed and could not move her legs below the knees.

OLYMPICS FACT FILE

The Olympic Games were first held in Olympia, in ancient Greece, around 3,000 years ago. They took place every four years until they were abolished in 393 CE.

A Frenchman called Pierre de Coubertin (1863–1937) revived the Games, and the first modern Olympics were held in Athens in 1896.

The modern Games have been held every four years since 1896, except in 1916, 1940 and 1944, due to war. Special 10th-anniversary Games took place in 1906.

The symbol of the Olympic Games is five interlocking colored rings. Together, they represent the five original continents from which athletes came to compete in the Games.

ARCHERY

People started using bows and arrows more than 25,000 years ago, which makes archery one of the oldest sports in the Games!

Each arrow must have the archer's initials engraved on it.

This archer is using a leather "finger tab'"to pull back the bowstring. Some archers prefer to wear a glove instead.

DID YOU KNOW?

There were no Olympic archery events between 1924 and their reintroduction in 1972. They have been part of the Games ever since.

The youngest person to win an Olympic medal in an archery event was just 14 years old; the oldest was 68!

If someone shouts "Fast!" during a competition, all the competitors must stop firing immediately.

A guard made of plastic or leather stops the bow string from injuring the archer's arm when it is released.

Arrows are kept in a special bag called a "quiver," which is tied around the archer's waist.

CYCLING, SHOOTING, AND SHOWJUMPING

by Jason Page

CONTENTS

Crabtree Publishing Company
www.crabtreebooks.com

Editor: Robert Walker
Proofreader: Mike Hodge
Acknowledgements: We would like to thank Ian Hodge, Rosalind Beckman and Elizabeth Wiggans for their assistance.
Cartoons by: John Alston
Picture Credits: t = top, b = bottom, l = left, r = right, OFC = outside front cover,OBC = outside back cover, IFC =front cover
Allsport; IFC, 3tr, 4/5 (main pic), 5tr, 6/7c, 10/11 (main pic), 12tl, 12/13 (main pic), 14/15 (main pic), 16/17 (main pic), 16br, 18/19 (main pic), 19tr, 21r, 22/23c, 23br, 24tl, 24/25 (main pic), 26/27 (main pic), 26t, 28/29b, 30/31 (main pic), 30/31c. Steve Bardens/ Action Plus: OFC. Adam Davy/ Empics Sport/ PA Photos: 8t. Image select; 2/3c. Robert Laberge/ Getty Images: 7tr. Phil Noble/ PA Archive/ PA Photos: 15b. Reuters/ Mike Finn-Kelcey: 20. Sipa Press/ Rex Features: 9l, 11b. Michael Steele/ EMPICS Sport/ PA Photos: 28t.
Picture research by Image Select.

Library and Archives Canada Cataloguing in Publication

Page, Jason
  Cycling, shooting, and show jumping / Jason Page.

(The Olympic sports)
Includes index.
ISBN 978-0-7787-4013-1 (bound).--ISBN 978-0-7787-4030-8 (pbk.)

1. Sports--Juvenile literature. 2. Olympics--Juvenile literature.
I. Title. II. Series: Page, Jason. Olympic sports.

GV721.53.P33 2008   j796   C2008-901005-1

Library of Congress Cataloging-in-Publication Data

Page, Jason.
  Cycling, shooting, and show jumping / Jason Page.
    p. cm. -- (The Olympic sports)
  Includes index.
  ISBN-13: 978-0-7787-4013-1 (rlb)
  ISBN-10: 0-7787-4013-7 (rlb)
  ISBN-13: 978-0-7787-4030-8 (pb)
  ISBN-10: 0-7787-4030-7 (pb)
  1. Olympics--Juvenile literature. 2. Sports--Juvenile literature.
I. Title. II. Series.

GV721.53.P34 2008
796--dc22
                                        2008005102

Crabtree Publishing Company
www.crabtreebooks.com   1-800-387-7650

Published in Canada   **Published in the United States**
Crabtree Publishing   Crabtree Publishing
616 Welland Ave.   PMB16A
St. Catharines, Ontario   350 Fifth Ave., Suite 3308
L2M 5V6   New York, NY 10118

ANCIENT ORIGINS

This book covers very different events at the Olympics. Some are all about strength. Others require great accuracy.

ANCIENT ORIGINS

Many of the modern Olympic events are actually thousands of years old. For example, the ancient Greeks held weightlifting competitions using huge heavy stones, while the first sporting events involving horses were chariot races. This Assyrian carving of a chariot rider is more than 2,500 years old.

GAMES EVERYWHERE

The Olympic events in this book will be held at a wide range of venues in Beijing, from the velodrome (cycle track) to the shooting range hall, and the archery field to the equestrian venues. There will even be a bicycle motocross (BMX) venue.

SUPER STATS

Only 211 competitors took part in the 1896 Olympics. For the 2008 Games in Beijing, more than 10,500 athletes will be hoping to win a medal.

RACE AGAINST THE CLOCK

Each competitor has to fire a certain number of arrows at the target within a set time. In the individual events, the archers are given 40 seconds to fire each arrow; in the doubles competitions, the firing time is reduced to 20 seconds per arrow.

The archer uses an adjustable sight (called a "bowsight") to aim at the target.

IT'S A LONG SHOT!

Archery events were included in the Olympics for the first time in 1900. Over the years there have been many different archery events, including some that involved shooting moving targets. At the Games in Beijing, all the archers will aim for fixed targets placed 76 yards (69.5m) away.

Olympic archery targets

This stabilizer balances the bow, helping the archer to hold it steady.

A woman's bow must weigh more than 33 pounds (15 kg), while the bow used by men must weigh at least 48.5 (22 kg) pounds.

TAKE A BOW

Olympic archers use a bow known as a "recurve" bow, which has ends that bend away from the archer. This type of bow was invented about 3500 years ago.

ANIMAL OLYMPIANS

The appropriately named archerfish would be aiming for a gold medal at the Animal Olympics. It can shoot a drop of water from its mouth over 1 yard a (0.9m) way with incredible accuracy.

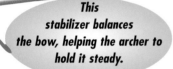

ARCHERY (CONTINUED)

Archers need both physical and mental strength. Lifting the heavy bow and drawing back the tight bowstring requires strong muscles, while great powers of concentration are needed to focus on the target.

An archery target has five colored circles. Each is worth a different number of points. The closer an arrow is to the center, the more points the archer scores.

SPORT FOR ALL

In 1984, Neroli Fairhall (NZL) made Olympic history when she took part in the women's archery event — she was the first athlete in a wheelchair ever to compete at the Olympic Games. Disabled athletes also have their own Games called the Paralympics, which will be held in Beijing two weeks after the Olympic Games.

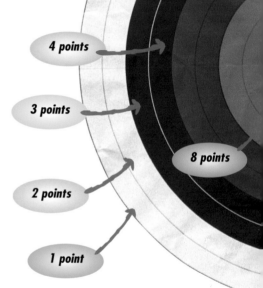

4 points

3 points

8 points

2 points

1 point

SUPER STATS

Once fired, arrows travel through the air at around 149 MPH (239.8 km/h) — that's faster than the average speed of a Formula One racing car!

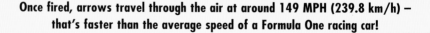

ITALIAN DEADEYE

At the Athens Olympics in 2004, Marco Galiazzo became the first Italian to win a gold medal in the individual Men's archery. The 21-year-old beat Hiroshi Yamamoto (JPN) by two points, winning the match 111–109. Galiazzo said he had worked hard on his archery for four years to be his best. He also said it might take him another four years for him to realize that he really had won a gold medal.

Marco Galiazzo (ITA)

Bull's-eye: 10 points

9 points

5 points

6 points

7 points

DID YOU KNOW

Another word for archery is "toxophily."

Disabled athletes will compete in 18 different Olympic sports at the Paralympics in Beijing. It will be the thirteenth time these Games have been held.

If an arrow hits the line between two scoring bands on the target, the higher score is awarded.

TAKING AIM

The archery target measures 1.33 yards (1.2m) across — that's about the same height as an average eight-year-old. However, from where the archers are standing, the target looks the same size as a thumb tack held at arm's length!

RIDE ON!

Gunn-Rita Dahle (NOR), pictured left, is the front runner in the Women's mountain bike event after winning the gold medal at the 2004 Olympics.Competition will be tough, with number-one ranked rider in the world Irina Kalentieva (RUS) and Sabine Spitz (GER) picked as favorites.

Julien Absalon (FRA) is the 2004 Olympic champion and a strong contender for a medal at the 2008 Games.

The handlebars on a mountain bike are usually straight. There's no bell, but there are two powerful brakes!

DID YOU KNOW?

Mountain bikes have up to 24 gears and some bikes are also fitted with rear shock absorbers.

The first purpose- built mountain bike went on sale in 1981. Now, 70 percent of all bikes sold are mountain bikes!

Cyclists in the mountain bike events are not allowed to deliberately get in each other's way and must allow faster competitors to overtake them.

ON TRACK FOR VICTORY

The mountain bike events will be held on Beijing's Laoshan mountain, on a course that's almost 3 miles (4.8 km) long. Each lap will provide the competitors with a zigzagging and sloping track to challenge their skills and fitness. Usually, the men race between 25–31 miles (40.2–49.9 km) and the women 19-25 miles (30.6–40.2 km). The exact distance is decided the night before the race.

Mountain bikes are fitted with fork-like front suspension help absorb bumps and knocks.

The tires on mountain bikes have deep treads to grip the slippery mud and are much wider than the tires used in other cycling events.

MOUNTAIN BIKING

Mountain bike events are like cross-country running races — only on bikes! Mountain biking is a very new cycle sport and is making only its third appearance at the Games.

ANIMAL OLYMPIANS

When it comes to tackling tough terrain, the undisputed champion in the animal kingdom is a small, goat-like antelope called the chamois. It can race up a rugged mountain, climbing over 3000 feet (914.4m) in just 15 minutes.

A mountain bike's frame is similar in design to a road or track bike but is made of stronger materials designed to withstand the tough terrain.

NO HELP AT ALL

Unlike other cycling sports, mountain bikers are not allowed to receive any help or assistance during the race. If their bikes get damaged, they have to repair them themselves.

Julien Absalon (FRA)

Women's: Gunn-Rita Dahle (NOR)

CYCLING

For the road race and time trials, Olympic cyclists will take to Beijing's urban cycling track, which is surrounded by 24 new public parks and reforested land.

RIDING IN THE SLIPSTREAM

Cyclists in the road races usually ride together in tight packs so that they can use the rider in front of them as a windbreak. This means they don't have to pedal quite so hard to keep up! The technique, known as 'drafting,' is forbidden in the time trial races.

Men's individual road race

SUPER STATS

The longest ever road race was held at the 1912 Games in Stockholm. It was almost 200 miles (321.9 km) long — that's like cycling from Buffalo to Cleveland!

TIME TRIAL

In the time trials, competitors start the ra one at a time, with a gap of 90 seconds between each rider. The winner is the cyclist who completes t course in the fastest time, not the one wl reaches the finish first. The men's event 28.5 miles (45.9 km) long and the women's is 19.4 miles (31.2 km) long

ON YER BIKE!

The bikes that are used in road races are much lighter than mountain bikes, and they have much narrower tires. The handlebars are curved, enabling riders to lean forward in the saddle, reducing wind resistance and increasing their speed. Road race bikes have eight gears.

DID YOU KNOW?

§ Cyclists on the same national team are allowed to share food and swap tools during the road race!

§ In both the road race and the time trials, support vehicles may follow the riders and help carry out any emergency repairs to their bikes.

§ At the 1896 Olympics the road race was won by a Greek rider who borrowed a bike from a spectator after crashing

The 2004 Women's time trials champion is Leontien Zijlaard-van Moorsel (NED).

ROAD RACE

The road races are straightforward — but very long! All of the competitors start at the same time and the winner is the first to cross the finish line. Each lap of the course is 11.2 miles (18 km). Men complete 13 laps (145 miles/233.4 km) and women complete 7 laps (78.4 miles/126.2 km).

ontien Zijlaard-van Moorsel (NED)

Women's road race: Sara Carrigan (AUS) **Women's time trial**: Leontien Zijlaard-van Moorsel (NED)

INSIDE THE DROME

All the track events are held in a cycling track called a "velodrome." The surface of the velodrome is made of wood, and it slopes so that the outside of the track is much higher than the inside. One lap of the velodrome is about 273 yards (249.6m).

Velodrome, 1996 Olympics

DID YOU KNOW?

Cycling is one of only five sports that have been included in every modern Olympic Games.

Cycling and canoeing are the only Olympic events that are timed to one-thousandth of a second!

The velodrome used in the 1964 Olympics in Tokyo cost almost $1 million to build. It was only used for four days before it was knocked down!

Chris Boardman (GBR) won the Men's individual pursuit at the 1992 Games.

The seat on Boardman's bike was higher than the handlebars.

To help reduce drag, the back wheel on most track bikes is solid (it's known as a "disc wheel"), while the front wheel usually has just three spokes.

CYCLING (CONTINUED)

There are 12 "track" events for cyclists at this year's Games — four for women and eight for men.

Track riders wear aerodynamic helmets designed to reduce wind-resistance (known as "drag") and help them travel faster.

NAME THAT RACE

Individual pursuit — two riders start on opposite sides of the track with the aim of catching their opponent. If, after 16 laps (12 laps in the women's event), neither rider has been caught, the cyclist who crosses his own finish line first is the winner.

Team pursuit — similar to the individual pursuit, except that this race is contested by two teams of four riders each. Only men compete in this event.

Points race — competitors race for 160 laps (100 laps in the women's event). At the end of every tenth lap, they are awarded points according to their positions: five for first, three for second, two for third, and one for fourth. The winner is the rider with the most points.

Madison — a team version of the points race, for men only, which takes place over 240 laps. The two-man teams are usually made up of a sprinter and a long-distance cyclist who take turns racing against the opposing team.

SUPER STATS

France has won 82 medals in the Olympic cycling events, including 39 golds — that's more than any other nation! In second place, with 58 medals, is Italy, while Great Britain is third with 46.

Women's points race: Olga Slyusareva (RUS)
Women's individual pursuit: Sarah Ulmer (NZL)

CYCLING
(CONTINUED)

The remaining track events are all time trials or sprints. Time trials focus on speed, while sprints test riders' cunning as well as their strength.

BATTLE OF WITS

Sprinters, such as Olympic champion Jens Fielder (GER), use cunning tactics to win. The riders usually begin very slowly and may even stop on the second lap in an attempt to get into the best position for the sudden race to the finish.

ANIMAL OLYMPIANS

Jens Fielder achieved a new record speed of over 43 MPH (69.2 km/h) during the 1992 Olympics, but that's nothing compared to the top speed of a sprinting cheetah. These super-speedy big cats can race along at around 62 MPH (100 km/h).

Jens Fielder (GER)

NAME THAT RACE

Time trial — cyclists race against the clock, and the rider with the fastest time wins. The men's race is four laps, and the women's race is two laps.

Sprint — a three-lap race between two riders. However, the riders spend the first two lap,s jockeying for position before making a final dash over the last 200 metres to the finish line.

Olympic sprint — two three-man teams race against each other over three laps and the fastest team wins. Only men compete in this event.

Keirin — for men only, this is an eight-lap race, but competitors remain behind a motorbike for the first 5.5 laps. The motorbike gradually speeds up from 25 km/h to 40 km/h before leaving the track and allowing the cyclists to sprint to the finish.

NO BRAKES!

The bikes used in track events don't have any brakes! They also have just one gear. This means that cyclists must pedal all the time to keep moving.

2004 time trials Olympic champion Chris Hoy (GBR) holds up the gold medal that he won at the 2004 games.

DID YOU KNOW?

The 1896 Olympics included a 12-hour track race. Only three contestants managed to finish the event, and it was never held again!

Until 1972, there was a cycling event for tandems — bicycles ridden by two people.

During the 1964 semi-final of the Men's sprint, both riders stood still for over 20 minutes. Both wanted the second position, which is considered an

Women's sprint: Lori-Ann Muenzer (CAN)
Women's 500-metres time trial: Anna Meares (AUS)

DID YOU KNOW?

♫ When the Olympics were held in Australia in 1956, all the equestrian events took place in Sweden. This was because Australia's strict quarantine laws wouldn't allow competitors' horses into the country!

♫ In 1932, the course was so difficult that no team managed to complete it — and no medals were awarded!

♫ In the event of a tie, the course is rearranged, and the competitors are timed as they go around again. This is called a "jump off." If they end up with the same score again, the rider with the best time wins.

EQUAL OPPORTUNITIES

Equestrian sports do not have separate events for men and women. All of the competitions are open to riders (and horses) of both sexes. As well as the individual event, there is also a team event in which four riders from the same country compete together.

Upright

The showjumping arena is over 130 yards (118.9m) long and 87 yards (79.6m) wide. That's slightly longer and wider than a football field.

Showjumping arena

A FAULTLESS PERFORMANCE

In 1992, Ludger Beerbaum (GER) became only the fourth competitor in the history of the Games to win the gold after picking up no penalty points at all.

Ludger Beerbaum (GER)

2004 OLYMPIC CHAMPIONS: Individual jumping: Rodrigo Pessoa (on Baloubet du Rouet) (BRA)

SHOWJUMPING

...ere are three different horse riding competitions (or "equestrian ...ents") at the Olympics. So saddle up, and get ready to gallop into ...mpetition number one — showjumping!

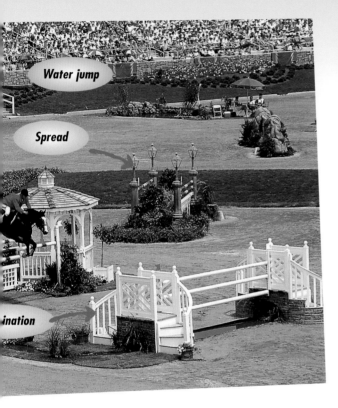

Water jump

Spread

...ination

IT'S ALL YOUR FAULT

In showjumping, horse and rider have to go around a course that contains at least 15 jumps. The idea is to clear all of the jumps in the right order within the required time limit, picking up as few penalty points as possible. These penalties are called "faults" and they are awarded for a range of different mistakes — for example, when the horse knocks down fences or refuses to jump.

LEARN THE LINGO

Courses are constructed using four basic types of jump.

Uprights — these are the tallest jumps and may be up to 5.6 feet (1.7m) high.

Spreads — these are wider than uprights, but also lower.

Combinations — these are made up of two or three jumps that are placed a few strides apart.

Water jumps — these are shallow, water-filled troughs that may be up to 5 yards (4.6m) wide.

DRESSAGE

The word "dressage" comes from a French word meaning "training," and this event is all about testing the riders' control of their horses.

DOING THE ROUNDS

The individual competition consists of three rounds. In the first two, competitors must perform a set routine of moves and maneuvers. The third is a freestyle round, which gives the riders a chance to show off their skills by performing their own routines set to music.

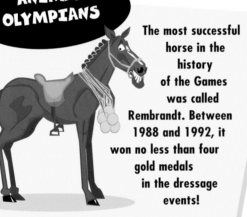

ANIMAL OLYMPIANS

The most successful horse in the history of the Games was called Rembrandt. Between 1988 and 1992, it won no less than four gold medals in the dressage events!

SOLDIER ON

Until 1952, only commissioned officers in the armed forces were allowed to compete in the Olympic dressage events. This rule was applied very strictly. When it was discovered that one member of the winning Swedish team in 1948 had a lower rank, the team was disqualified.

MAKING YOUR POINT

Saluting the judges, Atlanta 1996

Each dressage competition is scored by five judges who sit in different positions around the arena. They award the horse and rider points out of 10 for each move. Basic dressage moves include the pirouette (a tight turn in which the horse keeps one of its back legs in the same spot), the passage (a very slow, elegant trot) and the piaffer (trotting on the spot).

LOOK SMART

As you can see from this picture of 1996 gold medalist Isabell Werth (GER), competitors in dressage events must follow a strict dress code. This includes top hat and tails, a white shirt, polished black boots and white breeches. Riders who work in the police or armed forces are allowed to wear their uniforms.

DID YOU KNOW?

‼ Lorna Johnstone (GBR) became the oldest woman to compete in the Olympics when she took part in the dressage in 1972, five days after her 70th birthday!

‼ Riders are forbidden to communicate with their horses by making noises.

‼ Contestants can lose points if their horses swish their tail or put their ears back!

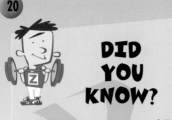

DID YOU KNOW?

In 1936, one competitor fell off of his horse during the cross-country run and took almost 3 hours to catch it again. He ended up with over 18,000 penalty points!

In the event of a draw at the end of the three-day event, the team or rider with the best cross-country score is the winner.

Riders must use the same horse in all three parts of the three-day event.

BIG BREAKS

Three-day eventing is by far the toughest of the equestrian events — as the medical reports prove! At least four Olympic gold medalists have stood on the winners' podium with broken bones. They include Wendy Schaeffer, a member of the victorious Australian team at the 1996 Olympics. When asked about her injury, Schaeffer replied: "It's nothing drastic, just a broken leg!"

BUSY DAYS

The individual competition is spread over three days, while the team event takes four days. There are four riders on each team. On day one (and day two in the team event), competitors take part in the dressage competition. This is followed by a speed and endurance day, and showjumping on the final day.

Leslie Law (on Shear L'Eau) (GBR)

THREE-DAY EVENT

The three-day event combines dressage and showjumping with a gruelling cross-country ride. It's the ultimate challenge for horse and rider and tests their skill and stamina to the limits.

CROSS-COUNTRY

The cross-country ride forms the final part of what's called the "speed and endurance day." The aim is to avoid penalty points by jumping the obstacles and finishing within the required time. The day consists of four phases:

1. Flat roads and tracks: 2.73 miles (4.4 km)

2. Steeplechase in which the horses must jump nine fences: 1.93 miles (35 km)

3. Flat roads and tracks: 4.92 miles (7.9 km)

4. Cross-county, with up to 35 obstacles: 4.6 miles (7.4 km)

Mark Todd

Mark Todd (NZL) won four Olympic medals in the three-day event between 1984 and 1992.

SUPER STATS

German competitors have dominated the equestrian events, winning over 34 gold medals. At the 1936 Olympics they produced the one-and-only "clean sweep" — winning gold in all six events. Switzerland has won 17 golds, and France has won 12.

SHOOTING: PISTOL

Are you ready? Then get very steady to take a look at the pistol shooting competitions. In these events, the slightest wobble can cost you a gold medal!

QUICK-FIRE ROUNDS

In the men's rapid fire event, competitors have only a short time to take aim and shoot. In the first round, they are allowed 8 seconds to fire five shots at five different targets. The time limit is reduced to 6 seconds in the second round, and 4 seconds in the final round.

Olga Klochneva (RUS) won the 1996 Olympic gold medal in the women's air pistol event.

Air pistols don't fire bullets. Instead, they use compressed air to fire a small pellet at the target.

A computer-generated image of the target allows competitors to see where each shot has hit the target and their scores.

ANIMAL OLYMPIANS

The sharp shooting star of the animal kingdom is the spitting cobra. When threatened, the snake shoots venom out of its mouth with deadly accuracy. It always aims for its enemy's eyes, and can score a direct hit at a range of more than 2 yards (1.8m)!

ONE CHOICE LEFT

Károly Takács was a member of Hungary's world-champion pistol-shooting team when in 1938 his right hand was blown off by a grenade during an army training exercise. However, Takács was determined that it wouldn't be the end of his shooting career. He spent 10 years teaching himself to shoot left-handed and went on to win two Olympic gold medals!

Ear protectors block out any distracting sounds and help competitors to concentrate.

Competitors wear blinkers around their eyes to help them focus on the target.

DID YOU KNOW?

Pierre de Coubertin, the founder of the modern Olympic Games, was a former French pistol-shooting champion.

Women competed in the shooting events for the first time in 1968. Women-only events were introduced in 1984.

Pistol shooters must hold the gun with one hand only.

Olga Klochneva (RUS)

ON TARGET

The distance of the target depends on the event. In air pistol competitions, it's 11 yards (10m) away; in the rapid fire and sports pistol events, it's 27 yards away (24.7m); and in the free pistol, it's 55 yards (50.3m) away. Each target consists of 10 rings; each ring is worth a different score, from 1–10 points.

Rapid fire targets

WOMEN: **Air pistol:** Yelena Kostevich (UKR) / **Sport pistol:** Maria Grozdeva (BUL)

Men's rifle competition (prone)

TAKING UP POSITION

In the air rifle and running target events, competitors stand up to shoot. In the "prone" event they shoot lying down on the ground, while in the "three position" event, they fire from standing, kneeling, and lying positions. Whatever the position, the competitors are forbidden to let their rifles touch or rest against any other object.

DID YOU KNOW?

♫ In 1920, 72-year-old Oscar Swahn (SWE) became the oldest Olympic medalist in any sport when he won silver in one of the rifle events.

♫ To a marksman, the tiny bull's-eye on the shooting target looks as big as a stop sign.

♫ The most successful marksman in the history of the Games was Carl Osburn (USA), who won 11 medals (five gold, four silver, and two bronze) between 1912 and 1924.

Marksmen are not allowed to wear clothing with straps, laces or seams.

BULL'S-EYE

At the Games in 1956, Gerald Ouellette (CAN) scored 600 points in the prone event — the highest possible score! However, his score never received official recognition because the rifle range turned out to be 1.6 yards (1.4m) too short. The first official perfect score of 600 was eventually achieved in the prone event by Miroslav Varaga (TCH) in 1988.

2004 OLYMPIC CHAMPIONS: MEN: Running target: Manfred Kurzer (GER) / **Air rifle:** Zhu Qinan (CHN) / **Small-bore rifle (prone):** Matt Emmons (USA)

SHOOTING: RIFLE

Six different events involve shooting with rifles — two are for women, and four are for men.

This black square blocks out the vision from the eye that the competitor isn't using.

MOVING TARGET

In the running target event, competitors have to shoot a moving target as it slides across a gap between two protective walls. The target moves at two speeds — on a slow run, the competitors have 5 seconds to shoot; on a fast run, they have just 2.5 seconds! This is the only event in which competitors are allowed to aim using a telescopic sight.

Marksmen usually wear a glove on the hand that holds the rifle but not on the hand that pulls the trigger.

Yuri Fedkine (EUN) won the men's air rifle event at the 1992 Games.

SUPER STATS

The USA has shot to the top of the winners' table in the shooting events, with 46 gold medals. In second place is Russia (former Soviet Union) with 29 golds, while Norway is third with 16 wins.

SHOOTING: SHOTGUN

At the 1900 Olympics people shot at real pigeons. Fortunately, the only pigeons people will be shooting at the Olympic games in Beijing will be clay ones.

WATCH THE BIRDIE!

Competitors in the Olympic shotgun events shoot at saucer-shaped targets known as "clay pigeons," or "clays" for short. Clays are catapulted through the air at great speed by a device called a "trap." The aim is to shoot the clays before they go out of range or hit the ground.

GUNS WITHOUT BULLETS

The guns used in other Olympic shooting events fire a single bullet or pellet, but a shotgun fires lots of little round balls called "shot." As these balls fly through the air, they start to spread out, covering a much wider area than just one bullet. This is why shotguns are used to hit difficult, fast-moving targets at close range.

READY, AIM, FIRE!

At Beijing, both men and women will compete in three different types of shotgun events:

1. **Trap:** the clays are released one at a time, and contestants get two shots at each one.

2. **Double trap:** two clays are released at the same time, and contestants get only one shot at each one.

3. **Skeet:** contestants move around, shooting from eight different positions, or "stations," on the course. The clays are released two at a time, and competitors are allowed one shot at each.

Double trap: Kim Rhode (USA)

DID YOU KNOW?

- Clay pigeons aren't made of clay at all, but from a mixture of limestone and tar.

- Clays fly out of the traps at 52.8 MPH (85 km/h) — as fast as a real pigeon can fly at top speed!

- In trap and double trap events, the clay is released as soon as the competitor shouts "pull!" In skeet events, there can be a delay of up to 3 seconds.

Ennio Falco (ITA)

Ennio Falco (ITA) celebrates his victory in the skeet competition at the 1996 Games. To be a champion in the shotgun events requires lightning-quick reactions, as well as super accuracy.

LEARN THE LINGO

Birds — another word for clays

Pull! — competitors shout out "pull!" when they are ready to shoot

Trap — a machine that launches the clays into the air

Choke — this part of the gun determines how wide the shot spreads

Cartridge — shotgun ammunition

WOMEN: Trap: Suzanne Balogh (AUS) **Double trap:** Kim Rhode (USA) **Skeet:** Diána Igaly (HUN)

DID YOU KNOW?

🏋 Many changes took place in weightlifting at the 2000 Games — the number of weight categories was reduced from 10 to 8 and women's events were contested for the first time.

🏋 Ancient Egyptian wall paintings from 4,000 years ago show weightlifters using bags filled with sand.

🏋 At the 1896 Olympic Games there was a weightlifting event that only allowed the use of one arm!

THE SNATCH

In the snatch, competitors must lift the weights above their heads in one single movement. As they hoist the weights above them, they squat down underneath it and lock their arms. Then, keeping the weights at arm's length above their heads, they stand up straight. Three-time Olympic champion Naim Suleymanoglu (TUR), above), shows how it's done.

THE CLEAN & JERK

In the clean and jerk event, competitors lift the weights above their heads in two stages. First, they raise the bars onto their chests — this must be done in a single, "clean" movement. Then, they thrust the bar over their heads with a quick "jerk" movement and stand up straight.

MEN'S WEIGHTLIFTING

The mighty weightlifters are the strongest competitors at the Olympic Games.

WEIGHT FOR IT!

Weightlifters at the Olympics compete in different weight classes, according to how heavy they are. However, the rules in each event are the same. All competitors must perform two different sorts of lift — called the "snatch" and the "clean and jerk." The heaviest weight that they manage to lift in the first category is added to the heaviest one in the second category to give their final scores. And whoever has the highest total is the winner!

SUPER STATS

The strongest weightlifters can lift three times their own body weight using the clean and jerk technique!

HOLD EVERYTHING!

Competitors are allowed three attempts at each lift. They are watched by three judges, who decide whether the attempt is successful. A valid lift is when the weight is held above the head with the arms out straight. The feet must be in a straight line, and contestants must be standing still. Sometimes the weight is just too heavy — the legs buckle, and down goes the weight *and* the competitor, as happened here to Manfred Norlinger (GER)!

WOMEN'S WEIGHTLIFTING

At the 2000 Games women were able to compete in weightlifting for the first time in Olympic history.

ANIMAL OLYMPIANS

When it comes to weightlifting, ants are in a league of their own. Despite their small size, these tiny insects can lift and carry things 50 times their own body weight. If humans could do the same, heavyweight weightlifters would be able to pick up more than 5 tons with ease — that's as heavy as five family cars!

POWDER UP

The part of the bar that the competitors hold has a rough, beveled surface to stop it from slipping in their hands. Weightlifters are also allowed to put chalk dust on their hands to improve their grip.

COLOR CODE

The different weights used in weightlifting are color-coded. When working out how much a competitor is lifting, remember to add on 33 pounds (15 kg) for the bar and 5 pounds (2.3 kg) for the two collars that hold the weights in place.

RED — 55 pounds (24.9 kg)	BLUE — 44 po(20 k
YELLOW — 33 pounds (15 kg)	GREEN — 22 po(10 k
WHITE — 11 pounds (5 kg)	BLACK — 5.5 k(2.5 k

Xia Yang (CHN)

THAT'S THE WAY TO DO IT!

Each weightlifter must hold the weight above her head until the judges are satisfied that she has it under control and that her feet are in a line. The referee will then give a signal indicating that she may put the weight down. Competitors must lower the bar to waist level before releasing their grip and letting go.

GREAT EXPECTATIONS

In the short time women have been allowed to compete in Olympic weightlifting, China has come out on top. Chinese athletes won seven gold medals at both the Sydney and the Athens games, and will be the team to look out for at Beijing.

DID YOU KNOW?

♫ At the Games in 1924, one competitor in the weightlifting event was only 13-years-old!

♫ The weightlifter Harold Sakata (USA), a silver medalist at the 1948 Olympics, went on to star as Oddjob in the James Bond film Goldfinger.

♫ After each successful lift, the weight on the bar must be increased by at least 5.5 pounds, unless the competitor is attempting to break the world record.

69 kg: Chunhong Liu (CHN) / 75 kg: Pawina Thongsuk (THA) / 75 kg-plus: Gonghong Tang (CHN)

INDEX

COUNTRY ABBREVIATIONS

AUS – Australia
AUT – Austria
CAN – Canada
CHN – China
CZE – Czech Republic (from 1994)
DEN – Denmark
EUN – Commonwealth team (1992)
FRA – France
GBR – Great Britain
GDR – East Germany (1949-90)
GEO – Georgia
GER – Germany
GRE – Greece
HUN – Hungary
ITA – Italy
IRI – Iran
JPN – Japan

KOR – Korea
NED – Netherlands
NOR – Norway
RUS – Russia
SUI – Switzerland
SWE – Sweden
TCH – Czechoslovakia (until 1992)
TUR – Turkey
UAE – United Arab Emirates
UKR – Ukraine
USA – United States of America
(URS) – Soviet Union (1922-92)
YUG – Yugoslavia (until 1992)